Introduction

During my six years as a member of the Chaplaincy team at Her Majesty's Prison Liverpool, known locally as Walton Prison, I became aware of the many evangelistic opportunities that were being missed by the churches.

Many people in prison are looking for answers, and if Christianity does not try to meet their needs then they will look to other religions or they will continue to use alcohol or drugs in an attempt to escape their problems.

Often people do come into some form of relationship with Jesus while in prison, but on release these new Christians find it difficult to find churches that are willing or able to accept them with all their baggage. I have often contacted churches to try to link people into a church community, but the silence on the other end of the phone has said much more than words could ever say!

The simple fact is that if the church does not surround these new Christians with love and support then they will return to their old circle of friends and soon fall back into crime, and their new-found faith will be lost.

In many cases this negative attitude was due to apprehension and a genuine concern for the existing church members. There is nothing wrong with this, as we need to act wisely, but sometimes it was due, perhaps, to fear of the reactions of the other church members. The biggest problem, it seems to me, is that people do not know what to do in this situation and they do not have the resources. This in turn means that church leaders are not equipped to grasp the opportunity that is before them.

> *People do not know what to do in this situation, and they do not have the resources*

The aim of this booklet is to look at some examples of work that is going on with ex-offenders and to help individuals and churches to become aware of where help is available for this area of ministry.

I will also be looking at how we can respond in practical ways, and how we can make the most of the evangelistic opportunities that are available.

Prisoner Profile

Sir David Ramsbottom, while still the Inspector of Prisons, said that 34% of people in our young offenders institutions have been through the care system, so we know that many have come from broken homes.

In a survey taken recently in one prison, 140 prisoners completed a questionnaire, and it revealed that the areas in which they felt they needed the most help were:

- Drugs   56%
- Alcohol   49%
- Employment   46%
- Housing   40%
- Education and problem-solving skills   18%

These statistics show the high number of problems people have, but also raise questions about resources. For example, a lot of money is put into drugs work, but the questionnaire revealed that alcohol abuse is more likely to lead to violent crime.

Also, if a person is to be successfully returned into the community, then an accommodation and employment or training package needs to be in place.

A number of ex-offenders have been in one form of institution or another all their lives so have become institutionalized, and on release they lack basic life skills. There are great opportunities here for church members to get alongside them as mentors, and to demonstrate the love of Christ by deed as well as word.

Check the Facts

We must also be wise. Although a person may have become a Christian while in prison, a lot of temptation has been absent, and often the real test starts once he or she has been released. If we want to do our best for all concerned we need good information. It is important to work in partnership with the prison chaplain and other professionals who may be able to give us information that we need.

Reaching Those Affected by Prison

Ralph Upton

Church Army Officer

Director of the Cranogwen Valley of Hope Project

GROVE BOOKS LIMITED
RIDLEY HALL RD CAMBRIDGE CB3 9HU

Contents

Acknowledgments

My thanks to Irene Summers and Ultan Russell for their help and encouragement and to Bob Spratt, Director of Missions to Prisons for his advice on content.

The Cover Illustration is by Peter Ashton

First Impression May 2003
ISSN 1367-0840
ISBN 1 85174 531 9

Go To Jail!

2

The Trauma

When a person is sent to prison for the first time it is a very traumatic experience and in the case of a woman it will often be many miles from home, as there are few women's prisons.

On arrival in prison they will be showered, given a number, usually given prison clothes and most of their possessions will be taken and stored until they are released. They will then be taken to the main prison and put in a cell, often sharing with someone they do not know. The sense of fear and isolation from loved ones cannot be underestimated.

Research by Paul Fenning of the Prisons' Inspectorate has shown that a high percentage of suicides and self-harm takes place in the first twenty-four hours in custody, so extra vigilance is needed by those caring for the person at this time. Reasons for this can be drug withdrawal or despair at finding themselves in prison. Those in prison for the first time are particularly at risk.

The next morning they go through the reception procedure, and one of the people they meet for the first time will be a member of the Chaplaincy team. As well as giving information the chaplain will try to assess, along with other professionals, how the person is coping.

As soon as is possible they are allowed a phone call, but I have seen newly arrived prisoners decline this as they do not know what to say or they find the thought of phoning someone too painful.

People who have experience of prison know the system, but it is a minefield for those who do not

The prisoner's family may have no experience of prison, and will be at home wondering what is happening. Often their minds will be working overtime, as stories of what happens to people in prisons go through their minds. People who have experience of prison know the system but it is a minefield for those who do not. Many questions arise: 'What can I send?' 'How do I get to visit?' 'Is he or she coping?' These are questions that families need to know and need help with.

Christians Sent to Prison

This is a very difficult group to deal with, partly because churches do not know how to respond and partly because of the added burden of guilt for the prisoner of having failed not only friends but also their Lord. Others in the prison will not understand this sense of failure. The continued support of the local church and the input from the chaplain is most important.

Often churches turn their backs on the person and this adds greatly to the feeling of failure. I write to one man serving a life sentence, and he often mentions, with some pain, the attitude towards him of Christians he knew.

We do, though, need to be aware that some people will seek to manipulate both the system and the churches by claiming to be a Christian.

Visiting

A visiting order is needed to visit a convicted prisoner. This is issued to the prisoner who then sends it out to his or her family and they are then able to phone and book a visit. Visiting is another very distressing time when people come face to face for the first time after imprisonment, and if children are involved the distress can be multiplied many times over.

In recent years, with the number of prisoners increasing, the number of visits has decreased. Part of the reason for this is that people are being held further away from home. The Prison Advisory and Care Trust (PACT) have suggested that increased security causes families to feel degraded, and the opportunity for enhanced longer visits reduces their frequency. Whatever the cause, less contact puts a heavy strain on a relationship.

The Prison Fellowship (See Chapter 6) prays for those in prison but also often gets involved in more practical issues. Some Prison Fellowship Groups provide transport for prisoner's families. This is a very practical demonstration of the gospel in helping to keep relationships together. Also applications can be made for assisted visits—normally the person needs to be on benefits to qualify, but this is not exclusive.

Often a person's vicar or minister may make a pastoral visit without a visiting order.

Families of Prisoners

This is a huge but, sadly, very neglected area of ministry. With a prison population of over 70,000 at any one time, together with prison turnover, people affected could be ten times that figure.

The Committee of Public Accounts at the House of Commons recently published a report on reducing re-offending, which stated that 'Active work between prisoners and their families to reduce the risk of family disintegration during the sentence is impractical for the 25,000 prisoners held over 50 miles from their home and the 11,000 prisoners held over 100 miles from their home.'

There are a number of ways in which churches could assist and reach out to this very vulnerable group. PACT say that many families do appreciate the help of a local church. The following list of key issues might be useful for churches considering how to help.

- Many families have problems related to housing, reduced income, harassment, debts, and coping in the community.

- They may have difficulty getting through to prisons to book visits, and appreciate help in their contact with the prison and getting information.

- Families often neglect themselves while worrying about prisoners and in some cases they go without to send money to prisoners.

- Children find it hard to cope at school and are sometimes stigmatized.

- Having a parent who is in prison can put a strain on children and their relationships, and this can lead to behaviour problems. Talking to children about a parent who is in prison is one way to help.

- There may be drug users in the family.

The Mothers' Union at Blakenhurst Prison has become aware of the effects on children of having a parent in prison. To try to help the child through this they have developed a scheme in co-operation with the prison education department in which they will help fathers to read a bedtime story and put it onto tape. The tape will then go through some form of security check and then the MU will hand it to the child as it leaves the next visit. It is hoped this will help with some of the emotional problems.

Women in Prison

The number of women in prison has seen a big increase, and if a female prisoner has children this can raise separate issues.

- Women tend to do short sentences—causing disruption, but with little chance of their doing any courses or training that will enable them to overcome their offending behaviour and to assist in their rehabilitation into society.

- A mother is often the primary carer, so grandparents, other relatives or the partner has to take on this role. In some cases Social Services intervene and this can be the start of institutionalization for the child.

- If a woman has a baby, even if breast-feeding, it cannot go straight from court with the mother. A procedure has to be followed, with input from Social Services and the courts which can cause long delays in the child joining the mother.

Making Contact

As with any form of evangelism, meeting with people where they are, both physically and spiritually, is the key. I am not aware of much structured work with prisoners' families from a Christian perspective. Many people have suspicions of 'do-gooders,' and in some cases prisoners' families could be living on the proceeds of crime. However, this does not mean that we should not try to engage with these families.

Meeting with people where they are, both physically and spiritually, is the key

The Mothers' Union and other Christian women's organizations are often involved in visitor centres, and could make referrals to these support groups which may be run by local churches. Literature could also be left in these centres with a contact number offering help and support. Maybe a group of churches could consider setting up a support group in their locality, especially if they are in an area near to a prison or in a geographical area of high crime. Prison Fellowship and Missions to Prisons can give help and advice on these issues.

One initiative run by Prison Fellowship is 'Angel Tree.' Prisoners with children can apply for presents to be delivered to their children at Christmas as if from them, *via* the Chaplaincy. Included with the present is a book that tells the Christmas story. A Prison Fellowship member delivers the parcels, thus making contact with the family.

Churches could either get involved in this or set up their own scheme, maybe even extending it to Easter. Some Prison Fellowship groups already give Easter eggs to prisoners attending chapel on Easter Sunday, so perhaps an extension to the families could be looked at.

Evangelistic Opportunities Through Pastoral Care

3

Pastoral care is very much a demonstration of the kingdom of God.

Although opportunities will arise from this, it is not easy to determine how successful this is as a form of evangelism. However, most people now agree that building up relationships is a major factor in people accepting Jesus as Lord and Saviour. There are a number of examples of how this is taking place in prisons and also outside, and although most of these operate through Mothers' Union or similar organizations, local churches might consider getting involved in similar ways.

Prevention

CARE, a mainline Christian charity that is involved in caring, have set up a couple of pilot schemes called Care Remand Fostering. This is a positive alternative to youth custody. The young people on remand are placed by the local authority in the homes of Christian foster carers, and the young people attend a daytime programme of education or work experience and some leisure activities are also arranged. The first pilot has taken place in Thames Valley, and work is advanced in Birmingham, Bristol and Colchester, with an aim to roll the scheme out there also. It would probably not be practical for a church to set up a scheme like this on its own, but as the scheme expands, volunteers will be needed from local churches to be foster carers. Sadly though, most young people who are remanded will end up in prison, and the rest of this chapter looks at situations within the prison system.

Chaplaincy Duties

The chaplaincy staff tend to spend most of their time providing pastoral care for people with many different problems. The chaplain is someone who is trusted. Inmates often put on a brave face when often they are coping very badly with a sentence, but there is a widely held view that you can let the mask down and be honest with the chaplaincy team. It falls to the chaplaincy to pass on bad news and to offer support at that time, and this sometimes extends to going to see the family of an inmate that has died in custody.

Visitor Centres

Visitor centres are reception centres where visitors go when they first arrive at the prison. They will wait there until being called over to the visits room. Mothers' Union members are very active in visitor centres. As people arrive, and often are feeling anxious about the visit for numerous reasons, they appreciate having somewhere that is welcoming, with some refreshments, and people to answer queries and provide a listening ear.

In some centres childcare is also available. This is very useful if some serious talking needs to take place without distraction from children. The MU is involved with this, together with similar organizations from other denominations. The MU is also involved in the administration and running of some centres.

There is always a need for volunteers, so local churches could contact the chaplain if interested.

Pastoral Visiting

I have already mentioned that ministers can arrange a special visit to parishioners, though such visits are normally only made to regular members of the congregation. Yet often if a minister hears of someone known to them in hospital, or of bereavement in the family, they will make a pastoral visit. As already described, prison can also be a big trauma, and the same sort of support can and should be offered.

Many churches have some form of visiting teams who might be able to make contact with the families

This can happen both with the family outside and with the inmate, although in the case of the inmate it is sensible to see if they would like a visit. I think people would be surprised at how many would accept a visit. I recently had a call from a clergyman who had a regular caller at the door, and he had heard that the person was now in prison. I was able to help him to follow this through and to make a visit.

Many families will be shocked, distressed and maybe even ashamed at having a family member in prison. They are unlikely to approach the church so it is up to the church to reach out to them in love. Many churches have some form of visiting teams who might be able to make contact with the families, and support them in this way. If we believe that pastoral visiting is an evangelistic opportunity, then this is an opportunity that is largely being missed by many in our churches.

There are some inmates who receive no visitors at all, perhaps because the family have written them off, or because they are being held far from home. The National Association of Prison Visitors is a non-religious organization but it affords a means for Christians to visit in the prisons. Prison Fellowship also operates a scheme where trained volunteers can visit people who have asked for a Christian visitor. Many prisoners welcome the opportunity to talk to someone who is outside of the prison system, to give them some degree of normality.

Many prisoners welcome the opportunity to talk to someone who is outside of the prison system

Mum's Night/Family Matters for Dads

In the Worcester Diocese the Mothers' Union has set up a Mums' Night in Brockhill Women's Prison. It enables women prisoners who are mothers to come together and to talk about their families. It also provides a listening ear if someone has a problem or if a child's milestone has been reached, someone to share and celebrate with, who shows an interest.

A similar project is planned at Blakenhurst Men's Prison. The MU runs a play area in the visiting area and it is hoped to target the fathers on these visits and to invite them along to this new project.

Parenting and Relationship Courses

Many people in prison have not had good role models in building and maintaining relationships. Many prisoners have children, and in some cases, children from past relationships. The breakdown of relationships while in prison is in the region of 40%. This often means that the children of inmates can go the same way—care system, young offenders institution, and ultimately prison.

In a number of prisons courses are now being run to address this issue. Some are run by secular agencies but the MU runs its own course in prisons. A course has been especially put together in the Liverpool Diocese for use with young offenders, looking at for example good male role models.

Sensitivity has to be applied when seeking to bring Jesus into this but obviously the links to a relationship with Jesus are not hard to make.

Support Groups

An area that seems to be largely neglected is families support groups. A Salvation Army Major told of one she had formed, and stated that it was welcomed and well attended. I have been unable to find evidence of schemes like this in place, although one Prison Fellowship group is planning to start one.

There is huge potential for a group of this sort where families of prisoners can support one another as well as getting help and advice from those running the group.

The Prison Advice and Care Trust, which has Christian roots, runs a drop-in centre for prisoners' families in North London and would be happy to give help and direction on setting up this sort of group.

There is huge potential for a group of this sort

Prison Officers

Most Christian activity is directed towards the prisoners and ex-offenders but there is also a ministry to prison officers very similar to the old style of industrial mission. It was my experience that once relationships had been built with the officers, they would talk about all manner of things, in particular the stress of the job. The chaplaincy team were also called upon to conduct funerals of officers and their families on some occasions.

Many prisons have staff prayer meetings, which are advantageous to many of the staff. However, officers' local churches have also got a role to play in supporting them in a very stressful job. For example, if there has been an incident in the prison the officer's family may well be feeling anxious about their family member. Also church members could consider working within the prison system, not only as prison officers, but also as teachers, counsellors, tradesmen or administration staff.

St Mark's Haydock is a large Anglican Evangelical church on the edge of St Helens, which advocates cell groups based around occupation where people can discuss things relevant to their own occupation. This could be worth considering in areas where a number of prison officers work.

Evangelism in Prison

4

Alpha in Prison

In 1997 I attended the first conference on Alpha in prisons. At that time the number of prisons running some form of Alpha course was quite small, but that number has now grown to three quarters of the prisons in the United Kingdom.

Most people reading this will know about the Alpha course. However, one of the things I learnt very quickly while working in a prison was that the average inmate has a very different value system. Alpha in prison will need to have a very different starting point from that of many churches.

The advantage of Alpha is that it can be adapted for many different situations, and I found that the videos did not work well in Liverpool Prison. For example, in one talk Nicky Gumbel spoke about punting, not something widely done in Liverpool. It was much better to do our own in-house sessions, adapted to our audience.

The advantage of Alpha is that it can be adapted for many different situations

The opportunities in this area are vast. I used to have two local church people to assist me, and the inmates appreciated their teaching and they had a very fulfilling ministry. As with Alpha, or any similar course, people do get converted and are nurtured and followed up by the chaplain and their team, which often includes church volunteers.

St Mark's Church, Battersea Rise in South London, has put in place a post-Alpha group for those who wish to continue, very much along the lines of a normal fellowship group. It is a chance for those who have been through Alpha to continue to pray with others, to look at God's word, and to grow in the Christian faith.

Alpha Churches

Holy Trinity Brompton, like many other churches, realized the need for follow up after release. At first they attempted to link converts to churches that were registered with Alpha. However, they are now prepared to refer to any church that states that they are willing to take referrals of ex-offenders.

Amanda Lee has been appointed to run a 'Caring for Ex-offenders' programme at Holy Trinity Brompton, and says that over 350 people have now been linked to local churches. This sounds very positive, but there is a weakness in so far as it has not been possible to monitor how successful these link-ups have been. Some inmates are still to be released, and the whereabouts of released prisoners is not known.

However, where link-ups have been successful we must be aware that ex-offenders who have become Christians they will still have many problems to be worked through and will need a lot of support. As stated earlier, the minister also has a responsibility to keep the church members safe, so boundaries and guidelines for all concerned are very important.

To enable this, Holy Trinity Brompton introduced a contract document between the ex-offender and the church; this can be found in Appendix 1 and downloaded from the Grove web site (www.grovebooks.co.uk). This includes things such as church and small group attendance, expectations, and any areas of the church that are off limit. For example, someone with offences against children would not be able to go into the Sunday school area. But it is not a one-way document. The church agrees to meet the person from prison, give them a meal, supply clothing and toiletries, and help them to find accommodation, work or education as well as helping them to develop spiritually. When I first saw this document, I had doubts about this but I now feel that any church working with people with significant problems should look at developing a similar system.

Bible Study Groups

As well as Alpha courses there are other groups, led by the chaplain, going on all the time. Some of these are run as conventional Bible studies, but this is often not the most effective way.

We are in a visual culture, and the use of videos, both Christian and secular, is often more effective, with many secular films giving the opportunity to discuss issues that affect the group and also enabling sensitive evangelistic comment. The book *Reel Issues* by Ian Maher (Bible Society, 1998) is a helpful resource for this sort of presentation of the gospel, along with his Grove Evangelism booklet Ev 59 Faith and Film. Bearing in mind the many underlying problems some prisoners experience, these groups can often uncover deep hurts, and a structure needs to be in place to deal with these issues as they are presented.

We are in a visual culture, and the use of videos, both Christian and secular, is often more effective

The Emmaus Bible School, based on the Wirral in Merseyside, produces Bible courses for individual study that are free to those in prison. These range from a very basic level to quite in-depth studies, with a challenge to accept Jesus as Lord and Saviour at the end of each book. Certificates are issued and these are a great encouragement to people who may never have achieved anything in their lives.

Spirituality Group

A more catholic approach is being used by the Mothers' Union in Blackenhurst. This involves meditation and getting in touch with the inner self. The group is open to any faith and the meditations are done in a way that enables people of any faith to engage, although I am assured that most of the prayers are Christian. Classical music is used to assist participants in relaxation, then an Ignatian style of meditation takes them, for example, 'out into the desert,' where some participants may cry out to God to provide for them.

Christian meditation would seem to be a useful addtion to what the churches have to offer

As many prisoners are under stress there is a growing interest in Buddhism within prisons, as meditation helps people to relax. Recapturing and using Christian meditation would seem to be a useful addition to what churches offer.

Sunday Services

Most chaplains welcome the involvement of Christians from outside churches in the Sunday services. Their presence helps to give the service a more normal feel. There are also opportunities to take a more active role by leading the worship, taking in a music group or preaching. Testimony is also very powerful in a prison context, in particular from those who have been in a similar position.

I found that talking about things that the inmates know about, such as current news, and relating that to the gospel was very effective. Having previously obtained permission, the handing out of tracts and other literature at the end of a service is surprisingly well received.

Christingle Service

In one prison the Mothers' Union put on a Christingle Service in the lead up to Christmas. This is a very visual service, an orange and a candle are used to symbolize the world and the light of Christ. Prisoners who were involved were cleared by security, but their families were also allowed to come in and take part. This meant that the whole family was together and was being reached by the gospel message.

Christian Literature

Even though many prisoners now have televisions in their cells there is still a lot of time to be filled in. Many prisoners read while in their cells so literature is a good form of evangelism. The Gideons often supply Bibles, but other donations of Bibles would not be turned down, as there is a great need.

Testimony books, such as *The Cross and the Switchblade*, are very popular. Stories of Christians and Bible reading notes are always needed, and with very limited resources, donations of books are most welcome.

The donation of books could become a very worthwhile ministry

Often the Chaplaincy has a small library, but the prison library would be open to receive books, and this could become a very worthwhile ministry. If interested, I would suggest you contact the prison chaplain. One word of caution though. I often receive books which are very old and very boring. Ask yourself: 'Would I read this?' 'Would I give it to my friend?'

Kainos

The word *kainos*, meaning new, is taken from John 13.34 'A new command I give you: love one another.' Kainos is a Christian Trust in the United Kingdom that has been set up to operate on a wing of a prison at the invitation of the Prison Governor. They employ a Christian co-ordinator to run the wing, but prison officers maintain security, many of whom are Christians. Part of the prison is converted into dormitories for this project, each housing eight men, so that they are effectively living in a community.

Much of the work carried out on the wing helps prisoners to look at themselves and the effect their crime has had on the victims, and helping them to confront their offending behaviour. The wing is open to prisoners of any or no religion, but they have to be willing to embrace the programme. Prisoners from all over the country have applied to be included in the scheme.

Much of the work helps prisoners to look at themselves and the effect their crime has had on the victims

It is claimed, with some degree of confidence, that the rehabilitation programme that takes place does significantly reduce re-offending, though a group doing a review of the effectiveness has challenged this.

The aim of Kainos is, through its range of programmes, to bring about an inner change to those on the Kainos wing. Residents on a Kainos wing live in a Christian-based community and disorder and assaults are much lower than on other wings.

Kairos

Kairos means a moment in time. This model of evangelism is rooted in the Roman Catholic Cursillo Movement, and in 1978 seven states in America were doing Cursillo in their prisons. The National Cursillo office determined that these prison Cursillos should become ecumenical. A programme was put together to serve the needs of those in prison and the first Kairos was presented one weekend in 1979.

In England Kairos and Kainos started in prisons in April 1997 at HMP The Verne in Portland and have now spread to Highpoint in Suffolk and Swaleside Prison which is on the Isle of Sheppey in Kent.

There has been some debate about the value of these programmes within prisons but chaplains are very clear of the value of them. In autumn 2002 it seemed very hopeful that Kainos will continue, but there is some doubt around the Kairos weekends that are more overtly Christian.

In April 1997 the first Kairos weekend took place. It was an intensive weekend followed by an 18-week journey programme. The weekend relied heavily upon volunteers from all denominations. It consists of talks, activities, time to share personal experiences and to begin to understand the often painful backgrounds that prisoners have come from.

Ideally people make choices about how they want to live the rest of their lives

The volunteer team demonstrate the love of God to the men, and the fact that people from outside will give their time has a big effect. This witness from the volunteers was the starting point for the healing of the hurt and rejection that many felt.

The structure of the weekend is very broad. Meditations are read aloud and reflected upon, followed by talks from volunteers drawn from churches of all denominations. After the talks they break into small groups of six residents and three volunteers, with volunteers sitting between the residents. This can be a key time in the whole weekend.

Many subjects are covered, such as forgiveness both of self and of others, the making of choices both good and bad, and the breaking down of barriers—many people put on a false front to protect themselves from the reality in the world around them.

People may well come into a relationship with Jesus, but this is not forced. Ideally people make choices about how they want to live the rest of their lives.

Volunteers must have been through a weekend themselves, and are known as Four Day Volunteers. The name comes from the three days of the weekend and the fourth day being the rest of your life. Each person taking part also has a Godparent, whose role is to support the person on their journey of faith. In addition, during a weekend, as well as those directly involved, volunteers from all over the country send messages of support and pledge prayer support.

Volunteers from all over the country send messages of support and pledge prayer support

Kairos can bring about a big change in those taking part, and this can cause problems with the family, who suddenly find a person saying and doing things completely outside the experience of the family. To help with this, similar weekends are run outside for the families of prisoners. Women run weekends for the women and men run weekends for the men. As well as helping them to understand the change, issues that families may face, such as isolation, anger and hurt, are addressed.

Family days are held twice a year and the participants' families, the volunteer team, Godparents and project staff spend the day together in the visits area. The food is provided by local churches, and the families are helped, if necessary, with accommodation.

Handing on the Baton

5

Rehabilitation of ex-offenders is a big task, and the effective linking up of those working with prisoners inside prisons and agencies that work with ex-offenders outside prisons has been very sketchy to say the least.

The link between prison chaplains and local churches also has a very poor history. Despite the Alpha referral initiative already mentioned, it seems that prison work is very low on most churches' agendas. Many churches are poorly equipped for the task, in comparison with a prison chaplaincy that is well resourced by the prison service.

Effective links need to be formed between chaplains and local churches to give a more joined-up approach to the rehabilitation of Christian ex-offenders. One problem with this is the number of people held a long way from their homes.

I have worked many times with people in prison but I was unable to link them with a church on their release. This meant that they gravitated back to their old circle of friends and were soon back in trouble and returning to prison.

> Wayne was released from a young offenders' institution but had nowhere to go so ended up in a bail hostel next door to a public house selling cheap alcohol, as it was closing down. Wayne has an alcohol problem and under the influence of drink committed a serious crime; he is now back in prison serving a six-year sentence.

If ex-offenders find a church which is willing to receive them, some initial contact is needed so that they are not expected to walk into a church 'cold,' which would be an alien experience to many. Other churches feel that they do not have the expertise or resources to handle ex-offenders, but would be willing if they had some help.

> Phil and John both have long-standing drug and alcohol addictions. While in prison they engaged with chaplaincy activities and have

been accepted onto a Christian project and welcomed into a local church. Even though one of them has relapsed the church are still praying for them and demonstrating the love of Christ in practical ways.

Most organizations that accept people from prison will go in and conduct assessments prior to the person's release. This means that a relationship is then built up between the agency and the potential service user. There is no reason why churches should be any less professional in getting to know the person and their spiritual and other needs; in fact a tool such as the contract could be put to good use in this situation. We need to be aware, though, that what is presented could be the tip of an iceberg, and there may be many problems just below the surface.

Tony served two quite long sentences before he became a Christian while in prison, and is now part of a church leadership. I asked him some questions about his change of lifestyle, which can, perhaps, help us in reaching out to ex-offenders.

What were the things you found most difficult upon release and did you have any help or support?

Upon release the most difficult thing for me to come to terms with was learning to equate my new faith with a new lifestyle in Christ and not allowing my former life lessons to affect my decisions and behaviour. This is very strange when you have not lived this life before—it is a bit like stepping out into a new planet and wondering why everyone else couldn't see the truth that I had found. Also nobody would believe me, apart from a very small minority. All this was very confusing and lonely.

What were the main differences between prison chapel and the church in society?

The main differences were that whilst inside nobody thought any the worse about you and accepted you totally. We lived out the Bible as written in the book of Acts. When outside of prison a monster called 'religion' appeared, and denominational differences, even differences between the same denominations, were evident. This was enough to put anyone off going back. Many people I know who made a genuine commitment in prison have fallen away. It is only the baptism in the Holy Spirit that I received while in prison that has kept me going and nothing from the church.

Did you find it hard or easy to move into the Christian community? What helped or hindered the process?

Initially I found it very easy to move into church communities being confident of who I now was in Jesus. I didn't realize that most people had no idea at all about what the Bible tells us we should be towards each other. I very quickly found myself isolated, mistrusted, or thought of as being arrogant. I found many people wanted their ears tickled by a good story of my past and then assumed I was still that person!

It took me some years before I eventually realized the unfortunate sad state of many people I was now to call my brother or sister in Christ.

I found that many expected me to fall back, and their double standards failed to put out the Spirit's light, to the disappointment of many people, I am sure.

You were in prison for some time. Did you feel institutionalized?

I have been in prison twice, and not very long by some people's standards. My last sentence meant I served eighteen months. May I say that the first two months of any sentence are the most traumatic. The lengths of my sentences were three years for the first and five years for the second. These sentences would crush most people and I felt crushed.

Upon release I was fine for the first month but even today, years later, I can have bad dreams about the experience. I do not like crowds in cities and I do not feel comfortable with too many people too close in a room. I do still have problems, perhaps even more than I feel comfortable thinking about.

As we look at these answers it shows a number of areas we need to address if we want to disciple new believers when coming out of prison. The person will bring with them all the baggage from their previous life, but are suddenly asked to live a completely different lifestyle. They will need a lot of support and direction from the Christian community.

Another area that Tony mentions is that people wanted to hear his story. My experience is that people leaving prison are often put on the stage to give their testimony. If, as in this case, this happens too early, it can give the ex-offender a star status and put immense pressure on a very delicate new-found faith.

The prison chaplaincies that Tony was involved with were quite evangelical. This would not be the case in most prisons which tend to be more Catholic and liberal. Denominational differences would not be as evident in prison due to the ecumenical nature of most prison chaplaincies.

Finding the right sort of church for someone upon release is essential, and needs good relationships between local churches and the prison chaplaincies. Discipling is very much a part of evangelism, and support in attending church and developing a spiritual life is most important.

It is a worrying comment that people expected Tony to fail and he felt isolated. This is something that many ex-offenders have told me. Certainly we need to be sensible, but we must have people in our churches to protect these new Christians from such negative attitudes and to fully integrate them into our fellowships. If we do not educate our members to be open and accepting of all, then we are going against the very commands of Christ.

If we do not educate our members to be open and accepting of all, we are going against the very commands of Christ

Being in an institution does have an effect on people. They often come out of prison completely de-skilled and need a lot of help with things such as shopping, budgeting, and keeping their accommodation clean. Counselling may be needed to deal with any original problems that led them into crime and also to get over the trauma of being held in prison—which Tony concedes still affects him many years later.

Special Considerations

Many ex-offenders may have other problems that require help from other professional agencies. For example, 70% of crime is drug or alcohol related. A person may have withdrawn physically but addiction and the mental withdrawal is much harder. The local drug council provides counselling and support for drug users and would be a good source of help and advice on this subject.

The group that greatly concerns most people is sex offenders, and from my own experience there are a number who are Christians within this group. Some will assume that 'sex offender' equals 'paedophile' and this is not the case—it can also mean rape, underage sex or pornography.

You would need to give thought as to how to handle an ex-offender from this group, and a clear strategy would need to be worked out. Agencies such as the police and probation services, together with social services, should be consulted before taking on a sex offender.

Mentoring/Circles of Support

One way that churches can help is by mentoring of the ex-offender, but this can put a lot of strain on one person. Gloucester Diocese has just embarked on a new initiative entitled 'Circles of Support.' The circle consists of six people, with the ex-offender as the core person, the rest being volunteers. The volunteers undergo training and support to help to equip them for this work. Ideally they would all have different skills, and one volunteer tries to see the core member every day. They also link into a number of other agencies so they are able to call on them for help and advice when needed.

The Quakers are also using this model in Thameside, working with sex offenders. They state that 40% of sex offenders will have some sort of contact with a church on release, and this is one way of working with this difficult client group.

Holidays

The Mothers' Union arrange holidays for those in need, so holidays for the ex-offenders and their families may be a possibility. Many dioceses have retreat houses, so perhaps these could also be made available in this way, maybe twice a year.

Community Chaplains

Some mention needs to be made here of 'community chaplains' which is in fact a Canadian model of working both within the prison with prisoners and outside with the family. In Canada the equivalent of our prison service and probation service is combined and has chaplains working in both areas. This model provides a professional focus for the churches' work with this client group. All the chaplains work with a large group of volunteers and are formally overseen by a Correctional Service of Canada Regional Chaplain.

In the Autumn of 1999 Revd Rod Carter, the CSC Regional Chaplain for Ontario, visited the UK. Seminars on community chaplaincy were well attended, and generated a lot of interest and enthusiasm. In some areas working groups have been set up to take this model forward in the UK.

Seminars on community chaplaincy generated a lot of interest and enthusiasm

The Salvation Army has followed this up, and there is now a Salvation Army Officer and his wife seconded to head up this work, together with another officer operating as a Community Chaplain at HMP Swansea.

This is a very positive step, and first reports are very encouraging, but it would be wrong to attempt to say at this early stage how successful this project will be.

Support for the Family

The family should not be overlooked at this stage; the family dynamic will be changing, and this can cause a lot of stress and tension within the family unit. Many ex-offenders have drug and alcohol problems, and specialist support is often needed, not only for the user but for the rest of the family as well. As many of the other organizations may no longer be on the scene, the support of the church could be crucial.

Where Can I Get Help?

6

There are a number of organizations which work with prisoners and ex-offenders, but only a couple that enable Christians and churches to get involved at grassroots level.

This is not an exhaustive list, but rather a starting point for those considering prison ministry. An address list is in Appendix 2.

Prison Fellowship

Prison Fellowship operates through a system of local prayer groups, and they also get involved in supporting the prison chaplains in more practical ways—letter writing, visiting and getting involved in services and study groups.

The group work that they offer is in the area of restorative justice and lifeskills. The only weakness is that very little work is directly evangelistic, although it is implicit within their courses. Prison Fellowship are willing to offer support and advice to any church wanting to get involved with those affected by prison.

Mothers' Union

Although an Anglican organization, the Mothers' Union also has members from other denominations, and men can become members. They operate through branches attached to local churches. If there is a prison in the diocese then it is quite likely that Mothers' Union will have some involvement, and this can be a good route into some form of prison ministry for individuals.

Missions to Prisons

This is an organization of non-denominational Christians formed by Revd Bob Spratt, a former prison chaplain. People linked to this organization minister in prisons in many different ways. Help and advice is given in working evangelistically in prisons and they make no secret of the fact that they want to see the gospel preached and people coming to Christ.

They are also happy to put on training days for local churches about working in prisons and with ex-offenders.

Prison Advice and Care Trust (PACT)

PACT came into being through the amalgamation of The Bourne Trust, which was Roman Catholic, and Prisoners' Wives and Families Trust. PACT provides a range of support and will work with local churches. Operating mostly in the London area it has just appointed a full time worker to develop services for families in the South West. A freephone number is available for anyone wanting help and advice: 0800 085 3021.

Partners of Prisoners

POPS, as they are known, operate in a similar way to PACT. Their base is in Manchester and they work mainly in the north. They also operate a black prisoner support project which is aimed at ethnic groups.

Churches Criminal Justice Forum

This is a national network that has been formed ecumenically which has already produced reports and has run a conference looking at criminal justice issues.

The aim is that this will become a strong campaigning voice for the churches, together with networking and advertising of events that may be of interest to members.

Local Assistance

As we saw earlier, many ex-offenders will have multiple problems and it would be wise to put together a list of useful contacts and local professional agencies such as local drug rehabilitation centres and youth offending teams. Some churches may have problems using non-Christian organizations, but they will often have skills that the church simply does not have.

It is also wise to affiliate to your local Council for Voluntary Service or equivalent, who often provide training, support and advice on funding. If you wish to contact your local CVS, information will normally be in the telephone directory or available from the National Association of Councils of Voluntary Service.

Many statutory and voluntary agencies are now keen to work with faith groups on projects, so that is also worth exploring.

Conclusion 7

Could it be, I wonder, that unlike the sick, the homeless, the hungry and the naked, those in prisons do not arouse a natural compassion within people, to respond in the way, I feel, Jesus would want us to?

Whilst I was researching the material for this booklet I realized that there were huge gaps in the ministry Christians offer to those affected by prison. In fact the perception of what churches and some para-church organizations are doing is widely overestimated.

Part of the reason for these gaps is a lack of resources, as churches are engaged in very diverse ministries, and perhaps more co-operation is needed between churches, as there is much duplication going on. There are huge opportunities that are simply waiting to be grasped, and the local church is ideally situated to meet the needs that are here.

The Way Forward

I have been in contact with some very large and wealthy churches, but they have very limited resources for this area of ministry, and so partnerships between churches and para-church organizations together with the chaplaincy must be the way forward.

Pastoral visiting to those affected by prison must be given similar priority to the visiting of the sick

Pastoral visiting to those affected by prison must be given a similar priority to the visiting of the sick and the bereaved. Training in this area should be sought from organizations such as Prison Fellowship.

An audit of skills already available within the churches needs to be carried out, together with the release of people into a ministry that is outside of the parish structure, especially in the case of many mainline denominations.

Alpha and other forms of evangelistic courses are taking place in prisons. Chaplains and other volunteers support them and follow through while in prison but the problems I have identified occur upon release.

Effective monitoring must be in place to help prevent people getting lost after release. This could perhaps be picked up by Prison Fellowship or a similar organization.

Organizations that have been working with those in prison would need to be willing to pass on names to others at a central point who would then take ownership of this follow up. However, better resourced joined-up thinking is needed to see this through more effectively—we can take comfort from the fact that God is sovereign but this must not become an excuse.

Lastly, local churches could link into the prison chaplaincies giving help and support, and also be ready and willing to accept ex-offenders upon release. A local directory of churches willing to accept ex-offenders would need to be put in place. This may be more effective than a national one.

Jesus tells us in Matthew 25 that what we do for the least of these we do for him and prisoners are specifically mentioned. So we as Christians need to respond to this in an effective and efficient manner.

It needs to form part of every church's agenda if we are serious about proclaiming the gospel to all people

It needs to form part of every church's agenda if we are serious about proclaiming the gospel to all people and to be inclusive of all people. A lot is already in place but we do need to do more.

Appendix 1: Agreement

New Member ....

I agree to abide by all the boundaries set out in this agreement, which will enable me to enjoy and experience the life of the church to the full, protecting me and the other members of this church from my weaknesses, and allowing me to grow into wholeness in Jesus Christ (Romans 12–13).

1. I agree to come under the authority of the leader of this church, and will be obedient to him/her in all things under the Lord.

2. I will attend meetings/house groups as directed by the church leadership.

3. I will meet with my pastoral director regularly, and will attend services and meetings with him/her.

4. I will not enter certain parts of the buildings designated 'no go areas' by the leadership.

5. I will not accept invitations of hospitality where there are any temptations to re-offend, unless I am accompanied by my pastoral director or ....

6. I accept that there are certain people that will need to be told of my circumstances.

7. I understand that if I do not keep to these conditions, I may be asked to leave the church, and in such circumstances, the leadership may choose to inform the statutory agencies, and the church congregation.

8. I understand that the church will do its best to nurture my faith and help me in practical ways, with the help of the Lord.

Signed ....

Print full name ....

Date ....

Church Leader

We agree to welcome .... into our church, nurture his/her faith and care for him/her in pastoral and practical ways. We will agree to do this in all the ways set out in this agreement, with the help of the Lord in the power of his Holy Spirit, and to the best of our ability.

1. We agree to meet you at the gate of the prison on the day of your release, provide you with a meal and arrange transport to your accommodation or probation office (where the relationship with the member has been formed prior to release).

2. We agree to investigate options for accommodation for you, and assist you in securing permanent accommodation, where possible using organizations that specialize in this field.

3. We will attempt to meet your practical needs (*ie* basic clothing, toiletries, food) and encourage you to find ways of supporting yourself as soon as possible.

4. We will investigate employment opportunities for you, where possible using organizations that specialize in this field, and will encourage you to take up employment as soon as possible.

5. Where you need specialist help in drug/alcohol or psychiatric rehabilitation, we will encourage you to seek this help, and support you in your rehabilitation.

6. We will ensure that you are welcomed into a small group, and will appoint you a pastoral director who will be responsible for directing your spiritual growth, and who will be available for counselling and emotional and spiritual support.

7. We will work together with the statutory organizations responsible for you, including your probation officer and social services, and will do all we can to co-operate with them and help them in their support of you.

8. We acknowledge that our responsibility is to God, and to the congregation of the church, and will do all that we can to protect the members of the congregation.

Signed .... Church leader's name ....

Name of Church .... Date ....

Appendix 2: Useful Addresses

Prison Fellowship
PO Box 945
Maldon
Essex
CM9 4EW
Tel: 01621 843232
Fax: 01621 843303
Email: prisonfellowship@dial.pipex.com

The Mothers' Union
Mary Sumner House
24 Tufton Street
London
SW1P 3RB
Tel: 020 7222 5533
Fax: 020 7222 1591

Prison Advice and Care Trust
Lincoln House
1–3 Brixton Road
London
SW9 6DE
Tel: 020 7582 1313
Email: alex@pact.uk.net

Partners of Prisoners
Suite 4b Building 1
Wilsons Park, Monsall Road
Newton Heath
Manchester
M40 8WN
Tel: 0161 277 9066
Email: mail@partnersofprisoners.co.uk

Kairos UK
Chair Andrew Lusby
25 Hillside Road
Wool
Dorset
BH20 6DY
Tel: 01929 463 234
Email: andrewlusby@supanet.com

Missions to Prisons
PO Box 37
Kendal
Cumbria
LA9 6GF
Tel: 029 2049 3895
Email: trust@greenstones.fsnet.co.uk

Holy Trinity Brompton
Brompton Road
London
SW7 1JA
Tel: 020 7590 8238
Fax: 020 7589 3390
Email: prisons@htb.org.uk

Welsh Council On Alcohol
*   And Other Drugs*
112 Albany Road
Cardiff
CF24 3RU
Tel: 029 2049 3895
Fax: 029 2025 7057
Email: enquiries@welshcouncil.org.uk

Prisons Community Links (CLINKS)
15 Priory Street
York
YO1 6ET
Tel: 01904 673 970
Fax: 01904 613 756
Email: info@clinks.org

Churches Criminal Justice Forum
39 Ecclestone Square
London
SW1V 1BX
Tel: 020 7523 2168
Fax: 0151 327 1592
Email: dews@cbcew.org.uk

Emmaus Bible School
Carlett Boulevard
Eastham
Wirral
CH62 8BZ
Tel: 0151 327 1172
Email: emmaus@kingsnet.org.uk

Valley of Hope
21a Cardiff Street
Aberdare
CF44 7DP
Tel: 01685 873 716
Email: rhonddavalleyofhope@yahoo.co.uk
Web site: www.valleyofhope.co.uk